The Little
BOOK OF Hope

The Little BOOK OF Hope

ROBERT H. SCHULLER

THOMAS NELSON PUBLISHERS
Nashville • Atlanta • London • Vancouver

Published in Nashville, Tennessee, by Thomas Nelson, Inc., and distributed in Canada by Word
Communications, Ltd., Richmond, British Columbia, and in the United Kingdom by Word
(UK), Ltd., Milton Keynes, England.

Library of Congress Cataloging-in-Publication Data

Schuller, Robert Harold.
     The little book of hope / Robert H. Schuller.
          p.   cm.
     ISBN 0–7852–7553–3 (pb)
     1. Christian life—Quotations, maxims, etc. 2. Hope—Religious aspects—Christianity—
Quotations, maxims, etc. 3. Success—Religious aspects—Christianity—Quotations, maxims,
etc.
I. Title.
BV4905.2.S373   1996
242—dc20   95–19351
                                                                                   CIP

Printed in the United States of America

1 2 3 4 5 6 7 — 02 01 00 99 98 97 96

Hope is an important human value for dynamic living. Where there is hope, there is life!

Birds were meant to fly. Flowers were meant to bloom. Humans were designed to believe: in beauty, in love, in truth, in God.

Keep your heart right,
and your faith will burn bright.

A year from now you may wish
you had started today.

Any person can be successful on smooth seas, but it is the victor over the storm who gains true honor.

Life's not fair, but God is good. Life throws us a disappointment. And God responds by giving us encouragement.

We all need help at one time or another,
so don't be too proud to ask for it
when your time comes.

God is present with you, in spite of what
the circumstances might appear to say.

I would rather err on the side of faith
than on the side of doubt.

Forgiveness is where we encounter
God's goodness . . . face-to-face . . .
heart-to-heart.

A prescription for joyful living:
"Be good, be kind, be unselfish."

It costs nothing to buy a dream . . . and it's the best investment you can make.

Faith stimulates success.

It's better to attempt to do something great and fail than to attempt to do nothing and succeed.

The secret of success is
to find a need and fill it.

Do you need a rainbow today? Then:
1. Expect one.
2. Take time to look for it.
3. Enjoy the moment.
4. Thank God for it.

Nothing is impossible! Cut the word *impossible* out of your dictionary. Declare the word *impossible* out of bounds!

Let your dreams, not your regrets, take command of your life.

You will never win if you never begin.

The most important thing is living your life for something more important than your life.

Love is the power behind faith.

When every other element is out of your control, remember you can still manage your reaction.

I'd rather change my mind and succeed
than have my own way and fail.

Trouble is not always trouble! It is often God's way of making us lie down, turn around, sit still, pray, work harder, or start over again.

The real crime is not failure
but low aim.

The most tragic waste
is the waste of a good idea.

Say yes to what is right, no to what is wrong. And you'll find peace in your heart!

There are no great people in this world; there are only ordinary people. The only difference is that some people set higher goals, dream bigger dreams, and settle for nothing less than the best!

Make your suffering a passage,
not a dead end.

Success doesn't come through
the way you think it comes—
it comes through the way you think.

Be thankful for all the storms of your life that have blown out, blown over, or passed you by and never touched you.

Selfishness turns life into burdens,
while selflessness turns burdens into life.

Everyone needs a purpose to live for,
a self they can live with, and a faith
they can live by.

God's delays are not God's denials.

Everyone faces disappointments at one time or another—but the winners are the ones who refuse to let disappointments become discouragements.

Talent is spelled W-O-R-K.

You must take the leap of faith to experience God's saving strength!

Tomorrow will not fail you unless you choose to throw it away.

Happy are the believers,
for they need never worry.

There is no success without sacrifice.

$\mathcal{S}$uccess is a journey . . .
not a destination.

Your life is in the care and keeping of God, who keeps watch over His own.

If a disappointment causes you to slip, stumble, and slide back into discouragement, then lift your mood back up by giving thanks to God for all things.

Positive prayer starts with two life-changing words—"I believe!"

Inch by inch, anything is a cinch.

I will face my future with faith, for I have God beside me!

There are vast untapped resources of faith
and talent that can be discovered
only in adversity.

Aim at nothing, and you *will* succeed.

Happiness is having a hand to hold,
finding a heart to heal, and leaning into
tomorrow with love.

Striving for excellence is an act of faith. God is not honored or glorified by mediocrity.

$\mathbb{A}$lways look for the potential in today
and the beauty in tomorrow.

Triumph is made up of two words:
try . . .
and . . . *umph*.

Believe the best about people, and if you're wrong, remember this—you've only erred on the side of love.

Add up your joys and *never* count
your sorrows.

Today's accomplishments were
yesterday's impossibilities.

No matter how obstinate the obstacle or horrific the hurt, forgiveness is *always* possible.

Thank God always. Deep in the heart of gratitude is a gift of tremendous faith.

There will never be another now,
so I'll make the most of today . . .
there will never be another me,
so I'll make the most of myself.

Be happy! You are loved.

People everywhere are the same.
We share universal need—
the need for faith, hope, and love.

$\mathbb{G}$ive God thanks—even as you face trouble!

$\mathbb{P}$rogress is turning impossibilities into possibilities!

What appears to be the end of the road may just be a bend in the road . . . so don't slam on those brakes!

No person is too small for God's love,
and with that kind of love,
no peak is too high to climb.

Find a need and fill it . . . find a hurt and heal it . . . find a problem and solve it.

If you fail to plan,
you are planning to fail.

Grace is God's love in action for those
who don't deserve it.

Press on . . . obstacles are seldom the same size tomorrow as they are today.

C-A-N-'T . . . just another awful
four-letter word.

Remember: The eagle stirs up the nest in order that the young might learn to fly! Your trouble may be your greatest opportunity.

Success is never ending—and failure is never final.

Never look at what you have lost . . .
look at what you have left.

Tough times never last,
but tough people do!

The biggest problem you face
is finding yourself surrounded with more
opportunities than you can handle.
Give your best time to your most
important projects.

Starting is half the battle!

Success is not escaping problems but facing them creatively.

Failure doesn't mean you should give up
. . . it does mean you need to try harder.

Running others down is no way to
build yourself up!

Family is the key to success. Family promotes a safe place. It gives the freedom to dream dreams and set goals.

$\mathbb{R}$eal failure is failing to make the most
of the gifts God has given you.

If you don't have a vision for your life,
then you probably haven't focused in on
anything.

God uses life's bruises.

Try to turn enemies into friends. People
who belittle people will be little
people—and accomplish little.

Never forget—there is a light behind every shadow. There can be no shadow unless a light is shining somewhere.

Believe that for every problem, God will provide a solution.

You can go anywhere from where you are.

It's better to do something imperfectly
than to do nothing perfectly.

Faith without risk is a contradiction.

Happy is the heart who offers a friend
to the lonely.

Every problem is temporary.
Every valley has its low point.
Reach it and there's only one way to go
from that point, and that's upward.

Become a "do it now" person. The world is out there waiting to follow those who have faith to move ahead.

Focus on giving instead of getting.

Courage is something you can never lose—because courage is something you can always choose!

You can become the person
you want to be!

Success can be defined as bearing fruit (being productive) and fulfilling God's plan for our lives.

Love sanctifies success.

Let go—and let God make it happen in His way.

If you listen to your fears,
you will die never knowing what a great
person you might have been.

Welcome tomorrow . . . for every new
day creates new opportunities.

Just as you believe in seas you've never sailed, so believe in a love you've never felt from the God you've never seen.

Look for the good, and you will find it.

Possibility thinkers are incurably
obsessed with the creative notion that
the best is yet to be.

Select self-respect . . . not self-pity.

Risks are challenges to meet—
not excuses for backing out
and quitting.

There is almost no problem that
patience cannot solve . . .
and no dream it cannot push
to victory.

God can do tremendous things through
the person who doesn't care
who gets the credit.

Be inspired by God's nature: Storms always lose to the sun. . . . The sunrise always overtakes the night. . . . And the winter always turns into spring.

We are creatures of choice;
we have the ability to choose
how we will react to any circumstance.

When it rains, look for the rainbow.

It takes but one positive thought, when given a chance to survive and thrive, to overpower an entire army of negative thoughts.

We learn courage when we face danger;
we learn patience when we endure
suffering; we learn tenderness
when we taste pain.

Never let a problem
become an excuse.

It takes courage to love. It takes a brave heart that risks being broken to discover the joy of love.

A giving attitude is the secret to successful living.

Hope is not the absence of suffering;
it is living in the presence of love.

Bloom where you are planted.

If you want to live, you have to give. This is the key to prosperity. This is also the key to joyful living.

$\mathbb{P}$roblems are guidelines, not stop signs.

God does not promise skies always blue
. . . but He does promise to see us
through.

Bad times become good times when they bring out the best in you.

Nobody can do it alone. We all need
the loving support of family
or a caring friend.

Success, finally, is not what you have . . .
it is not what you do . . . it is who you
are—children of the living God!

About the Author

Robert H. Schuller began his ministry with two members and five hundred dollars in a drive-in theater in California in 1955. Today his face is seen by more people every week than any other religious leader in the world. He is founder and spokesman on America's television church, *The Hour of Power*, which is the longest-running and the most widely viewed televised church service in the United States. It was the first televised church service to cover all of America, and the first televised church service seen in Europe, Korea, Australia, and Russia.

Every year hundreds of millions of people are introduced to his message from the world-renowned Crystal Cathedral, home of what is today the largest congregation in the oldest Protestant denomination with a continuous ministry in the United States of America—the Reformed Church in America.

Dr. Schuller is the author of thirty books, five of which were on the *New York Times* and *Publisher's Weekly* best-seller lists. His lifetime involvement in architecture, psychology, theology, and motivation seminars makes him a true "Renaissance man." He lives with his wife, Arvella, in Garden Grove, California.